Published by Business Jigsaw Press

Secrets of
Successful
Complaint Handling

Clare Moore

Contents and Index

www.businessjigsaw.com

Introduction

We all hope that we won't get complaints. We run our service so well that our clients or customers will never have a need to complain. The harsh reality is that suppliers let us down, we grow our businesses and take on new staff, our people get complacent, and sometimes our customers are just unreasonable.

You know and I know that there are a lot of organizations out there who have not got complaint handling right. The UK National Consumer Council calls this "the Stupid Company Phenomenon." Systemic poor service and a chronic lack of transparency are the key characteristics of the guilty parties, with Financial Services, Councils, Utilities and Telecommunications firms heading the list of offenders. In a recent NCC survey, half of those customers who had been let down or treated badly said it

Secrets of Successful Complaint Handling

was just easier to go somewhere else rather than sort out their present difficulties[1]. This book sets out to give advice to any organization, large or small, public, private or voluntary, on how to avoid the worst complaint handling strategies, and instead maintain strong and positive relationships with your customers.

It was while working as Head of Customer Relations at British Airways that I realized that turning customer complaints around was neither a simple nor an easily understood practice. The pressure was on to reduce the cost per case and to automate complaint handling. I quickly realized that this approach wasn't necessarily good for business.

This book is written from a business viewpoint and seeks to provide practical and

---

[1] Source: UK National Consumer Council Survey March 2005

Introduction

easy to implement techniques that will reduce the number of complaints you receive, reduce the cost of handling them and generate more "ambassador customers". It is meant to encourage, challenge and refresh managers at all levels.

We will look at the five worst complaint handling responses in evidence today:

Five Worst Complaint Handling Responses

1. "Not my department"	This may be technically true bu it is a lazy answer and i irrelevant to the customer.
2. "It wasn't our fault"	Again, technically true but it i also irrelevant. The customer i now getting ready for battle.
3. "It's not our policy to do that"	Now your customer is gettin wound up. He has starte writing things down.
4. "I need proof"	Your customer realises that yo don't believe him and is no getting really upset.

Secrets of Successful Complaint Handling

5. "Our office is now closed"	There is no-one available to dea with your customer's complain He's walking away... right int the arms of your competitor.

How can you avoid making these mistakes and alienating the very people you are here to serve?

Here are five golden rules:

Five Golden Rules of Smart Complaint Handling

1. Don't Screw Up

2. Fix it Before They See It

3. Be there and Fix it Fast

4. Listen, Listen and Listen

5. Give and Learn

Introduction

By following these five simple rules, you will create a Customer Handling Policy that serves your organization well. It will save you money by solving the problem before they get expensive and strengthen the relationships with your customers.

Chapter 1: Don't Screw Up

Complaints happen when something about your product or service does not match their expectations. That may mean that your customer had unrealistic expectations or that the product or service failed them in some way. Either way, in the customer's eyes, you screwed up.

Why Customer Expectations Aren't Met

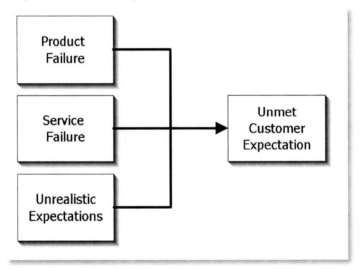

Secrets of Successful Complaint Handling

Let's have a look at what lies behind each of these issues.

Causes of Unmet Customer Expectations

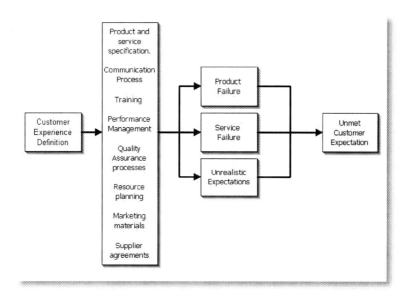

There are lots of opportunities to get the product or service wrong, or to allow your customer to have unrealistic expectations. As a business grows and more people are involved the opportunities to screw up expand exponentially. I recommend stepping back and designing the customer experience you want to provide.

Start with the Customer Experience Definition

By setting out what you expect your customers to experience when they deal with you, you are creating the framework for your product and service specification.

Map out every step of the process from the prospect hearing about you, right through the sales process, their first purchase, payment and consumption of the product or service. It should even include the process when they part company with you, because you want them to speak well of you to others, even if they don't need you any more.

Secrets of Successful Complaint Handling

Here is an example from a subscription based telecoms provider:

Customer Experience Map

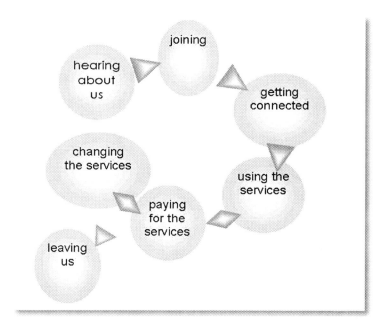

This overall framework is seen from a customer viewpoint. The detailed definition of each stage of the customer experience should include hard and soft elements of the experience. These should be defined by your customers. This can be done directly or using customer feedback, satisfaction surveys, complaints data and the views of front line staff.

Here is an example from a TV repair company of the detailed breakdown of one stage of the customer experience:

Sample Customer Experience Definition

Home visit to examine and repair TV equipment

Customer's View
"The repair technician was polite and helpful. He made sure I knew that all of the equipment was working before he left."

Secrets of Successful Complaint Handling

Hard Standards

1. Call ahead to the customer 30 minutes before
   the appointment to confirm arrival.

2. Van is in good working order, displays the company livery and is cleaned daily.

3. Check that appearance, uniform and personal hygiene all give a professional impression.

4. Toolkit and spares box is fully equipped and in working order.

5. Diagnostic and repairs process is followed as documented.

Soft Standards

1. Drive with care and respect for other drivers.

2. Remove muddy shoes and use portable vacuum to leave the customers premises as you found it.

3. Explain the nature of the fault using non-technical jargon.

4. Ask if the customer is happy and show them how to use the repaired equipment.

5. Take responsibility for any problems that may arise, do not pass blame on to other departments.

This definition can then be used to design training, to decide which performance measures to use, to create a checklist for each repair technician, and even in the recruitment specification.

Causes of Unmet Customer Expectation

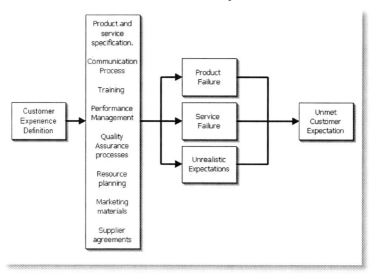

Once the Customer Experience is defined, we can tackle the eight areas highlighted above.

1. Product or Service Specification

The customer experience is the basis for the product or service specification that the customer bought, or has been led to expect. For example, no more than 3 people in the queue or next day delivery by 10 a.m. This specification then turns into a set of service standards that act as targets for the operational team. This can be straightforward enough when talking about the number of widgets in a box. It gets more difficult to manage when we start talking about feelings and emotions.

You may want your customers to feel comfortable. For example, a chain of tyre and exhaust repair garages may want female customers to feel at ease in their premises. Putting fashion magazines, a sofa and a coffee machine in reception is easy to measure. More difficult is the reaction of the mechanics to the customers. Women can smell a patronizing attitude at 20 paces but how do you measure it? Role play training can go some way to raising awareness and mystery shoppers and customer feedback can help managers to identify where the experience is not the one they wanted to see delivered.

Some hotel chains give their front of house staff laminated cards detailing the greeting to be used and pictures of table layouts etc, to remind them of the customer experience they are expected to deliver.

2. Communication Process

For a really big service failure, lots of people need to be involved, preferably not talking to each other. Typically the customer had given information to one department and this has not been passed on to another department.

Even in small businesses, as they grow, the consistency of the service delivery can suffer. More people are involved in providing the product or service and there are more frontline people for customers to deal with. Sooner or later, a process is needed to ensure a consistent customer experience.

3. Training

Providing an induction session for all new staff outlining the end to end customer experience and who delivers which part is invaluable. This overview can help your staff to see the implications of a seemingly trivial decision in any part of the process.

The product or service specification can also be used as the basis for technical and customer service training for frontline staff.

4. Performance Management

The customer experience definition should flow right through to operational and financial measures that can be used to manage performance.

Secrets of Successful Complaint Handling

Going back to the TV repair company example, the customer opinion of "Ask if the customer is happy and show how to use the repaired equipment", can translate to performance targets for each repair team. Using a post – repair customer satisfaction survey, questions like "Did your repair technician show you how to use the repaired equipment?" "Are you happy that you know how to use the repaired equipment?" can be used to provide regular scores for each team.

Where low scores are reported, the team manager can carry out more intensive spot checks, conduct coaching or raise a training need.

5. Quality Assurance & Quality Management Systems

Quality Assurance is the process of determining and verifying whether products or services match customer expectations. Taking all elements of the customer experience, quality assurance aims to establish effective and consistent levels of service. The Quality Assurance process considers internal activities such as design, development and production and external activities such as order placement, material procurement.

With the launch of the redesigned standard ISO 9001:2000 the term "Quality Assurance" has been replaced by "Quality Management System". This change reflects the broadening of the quality scope to include not only consistency and fitness for purpose, but to include customer satisfaction and continuous improvement.

A Quality Management System needs to cover four basic areas (Management Responsibility, Resource Management, Product Realization and Measurement, Analysis and Improvement) as shown in the diagram below.

Quality Management System

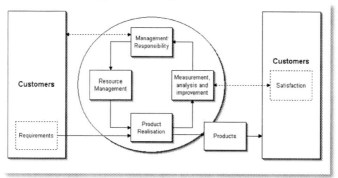

This "process approach" (using a system of processes within an organization) provides ongoing control over the individual elements of the business and also the business as a whole, and emphasises the importance of:-

Process Approach

1. Understanding and meeting customer requirements

2. Thinking of processes and activities in terms of the value they add

3. Measuring the effectiveness and performance of the results

4. Using objective measurement to continually improve the organization

At the heart of effective processes is a four step methodology known as "Plan–Do–Check–Act". This can be applied to all processes and can be described as:-

Secrets of Successful Complaint Handling

Plan – Do – Check – Act

Plan	Establish objectives and processes required to deliver the desired results.
Do	Implement the process developed.
Check	Monitor and evaluate the implemente process by testing the results against th predetermined objectives.
Act	Apply actions necessary for improvement the results require changes.

6. Resource Planning

The product or service specification together with demand forecasts and historical records are used in resource planning and scheduling so that the right number of staff and equipment are in place to meet demand. Contingency plans are also required for unexpected peaks in demand, staff sickness or equipment breakdowns.

Example: Resource planning experts

Many call centres have become expert in forecasting demand. Demand Management Software is available that takes historical data, demand factors, i.e. promotions/TV advertising and prepares staffing rosters to meet the estimated demand. Once staff have turned up for their shift, call centre managers have a number of other techniques to match supply with demand:

Resource Planning Techniques

1. Agents who are in "wrap up" are asked to take another call.

2. The callers wait in a queue until an agent is available. Hold messages can be created at various intervals during this wait period.

Secrets of Successful Complaint Handling

3. Calls can be overflowed to another team of agents. These could be agents working on another account in the call centre who have been cross trained on this service. This is known as a bureau arrangement.

4. Any planned "off line" time such as team meetings or training for the agent group is postponed until the queue has been dealt with.

5. Call control menus that offer options like, leaving a message or using an alternative contact method such as the website.

6. Team leaders or supervisors are asked to sign on as agents and handle calls until the queue has been dealt with.

7. Agents from other accounts who are finishing their shift or have been called in from days off are added to the team temporarily.

8. Untrained agents can act as a reception desk, taking messages to pass to the team, once the queue has been dealt with.

9. In the longer term, the resource level for the team is reviewed and new agents recruited and trained.

7. Marketing Materials

Most companies have ongoing battles between the sales and marketing teams and the operational teams over what was promised to customers and what was actually delivered. To resolve some of the conflict here, many firms now have a sign off process for all marketing material that will be seen by customers. The plans have to be approved in principle by the operations team and final proofs signed off again before going to print or online. This allows the debate about what is realistic to deliver to happen, before the customer is walking away in disgust.

Example: He told you what?
Many service failures occur when well intentioned sales people may have promised something was never going to happen.

Every company has examples of its sales people stretching the truth in order to get a sale. In a well known cable TV firm I worked with, the customer service agents told me about the "magic worm". When customers were worried about the cabling damaging their garden, an unscrupulous salesman has reassured them that, "our installation staff have special equipment called "the magic worm"". Apparently it could tunnel under block paving, cement and all other surfaces without a trace. Needless to say, when the installation crew arrived with picks and shovels, the customers were less than impressed.

8. Supplier Agreements

The quality management processes and schedules you apply to your own operation need to extend to key suppliers too. This is more and more important as firms choose to outsource parts of their operation. The outsource supplier is still part of the delivery team and all communications need to treat them as such.

Case Study:
A pharmaceutical wholesaling company I was working with recently had this problem. The shops they supplied needed the products next day. The wholesaler's suppliers would promise next day delivery but frequently fail to deliver. It was hard enough for this firm to get the contracts to supply in the first place but now they were in danger of losing those precious contracts.

Their solution, having discovered that none of their suppliers could reliably offer next day delivery, was to invest in a large warehousing facility. The cost of this new operation, while significant, was outweighed by the extra business they were able to generate.

It may not be our fault, but we'll fix it anyway

Sometimes, the customer screws up, and you still have to recover it to make sure they go away with a good impression of you.

This is a stretch for many front line staff because they didn't do anything wrong, yet they have to fix the problem. A good example is the generous return policy at Marks and Spencer. It is commonly known that people keep items for months and sometimes years before returning it for a refund. By this time, the item may have gone out of fashion and is no longer stocked. For the sake of the customer relationship, it is worth extending this policy for Marks and Spencer as it is an important differentiator.

Contingency Planning

Designing the ideal customer experience is important, based on what is important to the customer and what you can reliably deliver every time. Having this clearly documented is a good way to avoid the "over promise, under deliver" scenario. Go one step further and take time to think about all of the things that could go wrong for your customers. Once you have that list, start working out how you can stop that happening, and how you can get ready for it to happen.

Disney Corporation does this brilliantly. At their theme parks, they have taken note of the things customers do that cause problems. One example is that a tiny percentage of customers, in their excitement to get in to see Mickey, leave their car running in the parking lot. Even though it is a tiny number of people, Disney know that they can expect to see this happen. So, their parking lots are patrolled and staff switch off the engine, keep the keys safe and even carry spare fuel so that the customer gets home safely. They want nothing to spoil their customers' memory of their trip to Disney.

Getting the product or service right first time is the aspiration all companies have. For many of the reasons mentioned, we don't always manage to deliver 100% of the time. The next chapter outlines what we can do if something goes wrong.

Chapter 2: Fix It Before They See It

Most of the time, if you are close to what is going on in your business, you will realize that something is going wrong before your customer does. Unbelievably, lots of large businesses get themselves into the state where they realize they are going to screw up and don't do anything about it. Like seeing that their stock level is low and watching their customer come in and go out empty handed. Don't let this be you.

The Customer Relations team can play a key role in avoiding this situation. Acting as the voice of the customer, when they hear about an impending situation that will affect customer satisfaction, they can step in.

Real Life Example: Technical fault with Sky TV

Caroline Connor, Head of Customer Complaints at BSKYB gave me an example where they knew some of their customers would be experiencing technical problems.

Sky have a market leading product called Sky Plus that allows customers to create their own TV schedule. Despite extensive testing, there were some bugs in a new software release that was sent out to Sky Plus customers. Caroline's problem was that the technical team were not able to define the extent of the problem or how long it would take to fix. The new software had impacted something else in the system.

Caroline wanted to minimize the effect on customers and keep the level of inbound calls to the Service Centre under control too. She faced a decision. If she contacted all Sky Plus customers to let them know about the fault, then even customers who were not affected would hear about it, damaging the brand. How could she keep customers informed without having anything concrete to tell them about when it would be fixed? She decided to find out more before emailing the customers. She also briefed the service centre so that all Sky customer service agents would be informed about what had happened, should the customers call in before the fault could be rectified.

Let's look at some different ways to go about fixing a service failure before the customer sees it:

Fixing it before the customer sees it

1. Near miss monitoring.

2. Critical items (red, amber, green).

3. In the Customers Shoes.

4. Rent-a-hacker.

1. Near Miss Monitoring

In the UK, the National Health Service has recently adopted this system to track medical errors made in hospitals. The idea is taken from the airline industry where two aircraft colliding is not something anyone can afford to happen. Whenever an aircraft comes too close to either another aircraft or anything else, a "Near Miss" is recorded and investigated. The factors that allowed the near miss to happen can then be rectified before a real collision happens. In hospitals, the processes, training, information or human factors can also be addressed before a patient is seriously affected or even dies.

In your organization, I encourage you to look at the most serious failures you could make in terms of your customers. Sending letters in the wrong typeface is not going to make it onto this list, but allowing elderly people's power supply to go off for several days in the winter would.

Once you have your list of potential critical failures, make sure you have a reporting system that flags up incidents that come close to failure. These can then be investigated and action taken to remedy the situation before anything more serious happens.

2. Critical Items (red, amber and green)

More and more procurement and stock management departments are using this system to help them manage their costs. In supermarkets, bread, milk and carrots are included in the RED category. As soon as stocks start coming close to nil, extra stocks are immediately ordered in. The supplier contracts are designed for faster lead times and the in store staff replenish these items first.

In British Airways, boarding cards are very low cost items but critical to the day to day operation. Processes are set up to keep healthy stock levels and to maintain the boarding card printers.

Amber items are important but will not halt the operation or cause serious inconvenience to customers.

Green items are "nice to have" and more risk can be taken with stock levels to keep down costs.

When designing your Red, Amber and Green system of prioritizing, keep your customers in mind. Running out of a particular brand of mineral water in your restaurant may seem minor to you but if it is very important to your customers, it should be moved up to an Amber.

3. In the Customers' Shoes

One great way of spotting service failures before your customers is to actually be a customer. Get on your own mailing list. Get on your own prospect customer list. Walk around your premises before the first customer comes in each day. Try out the service or product yourself.

Real Life Example:

People who work in the customer service department often find out first about a new promotion when they get it through their own letterbox at home. They usually get a briefing from Marketing but sometimes the process breaks down. If there are errors in there, they can spot it and get a briefing out to their staff.

4. Rent a Hacker

For websites where security is an issue such as financial institutions, renting your own hacker to test out the security protection on your site is a good way to fix any weaknesses before your customers are stung. The same principle can be used where firms use Mystery Shopper services.

Here, companies like BPS will send their staff to be customers of their client's business. Whether they are travelling on ferries, staying at hotels or shopping online, they monitor the service they receive, often taking photographs and even video footage of their experiences. The results of this research is then presented back to the client firm and used to improve performance.

Tip:

If your firm is taking on new recruits regularly, why not send them as mystery shopping to your competitors as well as your own firm as part of their induction training? Not only will they find out more about the products and services, they are literally putting themselves in the customers' shoes.

If you want to give your team an injection of customer focus, how about asking them to make a 10 minute presentation of the results of their mystery shopping task. You could get each team member to test out a different competitor or product of yours.

Chapter 3: Be There and Fix It Fast

So somehow we have got to the situation where the customer has experienced a service failure. Could you have got to them first? How easy have you made it for them to let you know?

The worst thing that can happen now is that they walk away and never do business with you again...and don't tell you what happened.

The best thing that can happen is that they tell your people, your people fix it immediately, win the customer's goodwill back and record the situation so that it doesn't happen to anybody else.

Alternatively, the customer can accept it, not bother you with it and continue being your customer. Fewer and fewer customers are prepared to do this. If you are a monopoly supplier, the customer ends up feeling like a hostage and as soon as an alternative appears on the market, they're off.

Disappointed Customer's Options – and the consequences

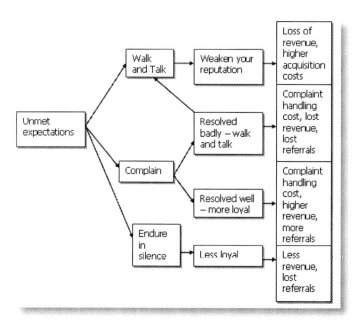

Where you have been unable to fix the problem before the customer sees it, there is a big opportunity.

> Research shows that customers who had
> complaint well handled felt more loyal tha
> customers who had never had a problem i
> the first place.

This does not mean that you should go around putting flies in your customers' soup!

It does mean that when you know your customers are going to experience a service failure, you get ready to knock their socks off with your proactive service recovery.

Case Study 1. Proactive Service Recovery

All passenger transport companies will face the situation of delays to their services. There is a lot that these firms can do to minimize the number and extent of delays, but they know that occasionally, they will still happen. Here are some of the ways to deal with this:

Secrets of Successful Complaint Handling

1. Pad the schedule.
Adding contingency time for delays is a commonly used device. If you don't expect to land in Frankfurt until 0830, then the 10 minute air traffic control delay that gets you on the tarmac at 0825 doesn't hurt.

2. Immediate and regular updates.
Train companies in the UK are now diligently making announcements as soon as the train has stopped. They go something like this: "This is your train guard speaking. I would like to apologise for the delay to your service. The reason for this delay is now being investigated by the driver. As soon as I have further information, I will let you know."

3. On the spot service recovery
Where you are unable to deliver the service booked, offer an alternative and an extra something to say sorry. Hotels may use a room upgrade, flowers or a bottle of wine. The restaurant where your 8pm table is not

ready until 8.30pm may offer you a complimentary drink at the bar.

Proactive Service Recovery

Getting to those customers who are not going to get their package in time or who will get orange socks instead of pink ones is important. Here's what to do when you can see a problem coming:

Proactive Service Recovery

1. Let them know what they are NOT going to get.

2. Apologise.

3. Explain why this happened and what you are doing to avoid it re-occurring in future.

4. Let them know what you have arranged instead.

5. Give them some choices.

6. Deliver on their choice.

7. Add an extra, unexpected touch.

8. Record the information on their customer record.

Secrets of Successful Complaint Handling

Your customers now have a story to tell their friends about how well your firm treated them when something went wrong. This positive story is going to build your reputation and win you more business.

Case Study: Proactive Service Recovery

As Head of Customer Relations at British Airways, one of the most testing situations I faced was a flight from Lusaka with a creeping delay. The flight was ready to depart when a technical fault was found in one of the engines. At first, the ground staff thought it could be fixed in a few hours. Then it transpired that a new part had to be found, flown out from the UK, and fitted.

With only two flights a week ourselves and very few other flights operating, there was no option to route the passengers on another service. There was very little hotel accommodation available in the vicinity of the airport, so most of the passengers had to stay on the aircraft for a full 18 hours. The food and drink supplies quickly ran out. The ground staff did a heroic job in finding more provisions.

By the time the flight was ready to depart the next day, the passengers were tired, hungry and very grumpy. The cabin crew did their best for the passengers with limited resources.

Meanwhile, back in London, the service recovery team had been pulled together. We had arranged new transfer connections for those connecting to other flights. We had foreign language speakers lined up to help. The baggage team were at the ready. We had refreshments arranged in the baggage hall. We had decided to offer every passenger a free flight anywhere in the world as a gesture of goodwill. Apology letters with the offer of the free flights had been prepared. I went along to the gate to

Secrets of Successful Complaint Handling

make a PA announcement on board and hand each passenger their letter.

The first passenger I met threw the letter back at me, shouting "I'll see you in court!" After that, everyone else I met was resigned, grateful to be in London at last and just wanted to get home.

Then I heard over the radio that the baggage team were unable to open the baggage hold. Just before they got stuck in ripping open the door, they managed to unseal the door and avoid too much damage to the aircraft.

It was a difficult and upsetting time for the passengers, especially those with children. We did get letters from some of the passengers later, thanking us for everything we had done.

Chapter 4:   Listen, listen, listen – From Tiger to Pussycat

The vast majority of customers are happy to give us feedback if they think we'll act on it – 84% to be precise[2].   Unfortunately only 50% of customers actually say they tell us before taking their business elsewhere.

Let's assume your customer is one who thinks you will act on their feedback. So the customer is complaining. They are upset, angry, and have a list of demands. The first three people they spoke to didn't listen to them, so now they are calling you. Are you ready to handle this?

In this chapter we will cover the following areas:

---

[2] Source: UK National Consumer Council Research March 2006

Secrets of Successful Complaint Handling

1. Giving your customer a way to be heard

2. The Marco Mindset.

3. From Anger to Information.

4. What you Need to Know.

1. Giving Your Customers a Way To Be Heard

We all love to receive compliments. We work so hard on getting it right, it is encouraging to hear how much our customers appreciate our efforts.

It is also human nature to avoid situations where you might be criticized. It is an unfortunate fact of life that most of the time our customers only tell us about the service when something goes wrong.

Which is more valuable to your business – a compliment or a complaint? Which is going to cost you more if it is not handled well?

Which do you need to put more effort in to find out about? We need to hear the complaints and so we need to make it easy for our customers to let us know what they are less than happy about.

Here are some of the ways we could open up the channels to hear our customers' views:

a. Senior employee approaching customer directl for feedback

b. Frontline staff asking "is everything OK?" or "Ho are we doing?"

c. Frontline staff passing customer to the manager.

d. Video booths to record customer comments.

e. Customer Comment Form

f. Email address for a Customer Service Department

g. Web chat facility for a Customer Servic Department

Secrets of Successful Complaint Handling

h. Telephone number for a Customer Servic Department

i. Mailing address for a Customer Service Department

j. Customer Satisfaction Survey

k. Customer Listening Forums

l. Corporate Hospitality Events

a. Senior employee approaching customer directly for feedback

Take a look at how often your senior people are talking to customers. In some firms, the CEO will hold Breakfast Meetings or Dinners for groups of top customers. The objective is for him or her to listen to what those customers think about the service, the competitors, to find out what plans their businesses have and how your firm might fit in.

Some firms have "Meet the Customer" programmes for their Directors. I have taken Directors around to meet customers on many occasions. Although some have been terrified of actually talking to a real customer, they all get a lot out of it and want to do more. It is a fantastic reality check for some of the initiatives that are being discussed around the boardroom table.

After your next Executive team meeting, how about each Executive calling up or walking up to a customer and asking them what they think of your organisation?

Frontline staff asking "Is everything OK?" or "How are we doing?"

Have you ever been in a restaurant and the waitress has come by and asked "Is everything alright with your meal?" Your automatic answer is "Yes." You would have to be ready with a gripe to say anything else. What about this instead, "Is there anything else I can get for you?" Now this is probably going to cause the waitress more work because you are likely to think of something, but it is a much more effective customer satisfaction check.

b. Front line staff passing customer to the manager

When the frontline person has reached the limit of their authority and skills, they will escalate the issue to their managers. Many customers nowadays will judge the competency of the person they are dealing with within three seconds and demand to speak to their manager immediately if they don't think the first person is going to be sympathetic.

So that the manager can manage, ideally your front line people are handling 95% of the customer issues themselves, perfectly well.

c. Video booths to record customer comments.

Most firms who have tried these have pulled them out again pretty quickly. It is different, it is innovative and it encourages teenagers to sit in there and send you rude messages.

d. Customer Comment Form
When we start to get into Customer Comment Form territory, we have to be aware of a few common pitfalls:

Staff may vet the forms and dump the negative ones. Really, this happens. You can include a prepaid envelope addressed to head office but it won't always get there.
Some customers are professional form fillers. The ones you really want to hear from don't bother.
You have to have someone good, opening, reading and responding to the forms, every day. If you don't, it is worse than having no forms.

e. Email address for a Customer Service Department

The key here is that the email will get to the right person quickly and will be responded to quickly and appropriately. If your systems cannot guarantee this, don't publish the email address until they can.

f. Telephone number for a Customer Service Department

Telephone help lines have to be helpful. Free phone numbers are good, premium charge numbers are bad. Adequate staffing levels are critical. Helpful, knowledgeable people on the other end of the line are also a good idea. Many firms get enough helpful friendly staff into the call centre and then fail to give them the product knowledge and authority levels to actually do anything helpful.

g. Mailing address for a Customer Service Department

Make it freepost and make sure there is someone good at the other end, who will open, read and respond to the forms, every day.

h. Customer Satisfaction Survey

There is an art and a science to designing, executing and analyzing customer satisfaction surveys. To avoid hearing what you wanted to hear and learning nothing, I suggest this process:

Secrets of Successful Complaint Handling

Customer Survey Process

1. Identify what it is that you really want to know. How much detail do you really need?

2. Work out how you are going to use the information. e.g. as the basis for performance related pay, as the basis for investment decision, to get someone sacked?

3. Go back to what you said for 1. and revise it.

4. Approach three well known and recommended market research firms with your requirements.

5. Review their responses and costs and choose the one that meets your requirements and a reasonable cost.

6. Brief staff that a survey will be conducted, and what their areas are that will be covered, without saying exactly when. Communicate how the results are going to be used.

7. Review the results and prepare an action plan. Thi should include a communication plan to share th information and your reaction to it with the staff.

i. Customer Listening Forums

These are great for getting to a detailed level of information about what your customers would like to see in the future. If you have widely publicized problems like an airline catering strike, then you can get feedback on how it was handled and how to improve next time. Try to design a well structured and facilitated event that allows for individual issues to be taken offline rather than being shared with other customers.

j. Corporate Hospitality Events

What are they for? Relationship building and information gathering – not complaint handling. Ideally, you want to find out about the complaints before getting to the event. You have lots of other happy customers there who are also going to hear a diatribe about the consequences of your late delivery performance.

Secrets of Successful Complaint Handling

There's a Problem...

These are all techniques that you can use when the customer is still talking to you. They assume that the customer cares enough about you to bother participating. There is one big problem here.

Think about what happens when you've had a bad experience. You don't go back. You don't call. You don't upgrade.

It is easy to measure activity, it's there, and it can be counted. Our unhappy customers are not talking and they are not buying. So start measuring what isn't happening and you start to find the people who don't care enough about you to get in touch themselves. It is harder to turn these people around but still possible.

Here are some tools to use to capture the views of defecting customers:

Look back over your customer records.

- Which customers have reduced their spend from the usual patterns?
- Which customers have cancelled their direct debit arrangements?
- Which customers have stopped referring other customers to you?
- Which customers are harder to get hold of when you try to contact them?
- Which customers have stopped responding to offers you send them?

Approach them with a call or letter to ask why they have stopped using your products or services. Assure them that their custom is valued and you want to bring them back as loyal customers. You could even include a "welcome back" offer.

! Warning. If you know that your firm is still grappling with poor service, don't encourage your defected customers to come back until you have fixed it.

Secrets of Successful Complaint Handling

Look for chat rooms, blogs, or fake company websites where your customers might be criticizing your company. Contact the complainers directly, rather than in the public forum, if possible. Check these websites:

www.complaints.com,
www.virginaircrewlies.com
www.grumbletext.co.uk
www.clik2complaints.co.uk

Go to Google, type in your company name and complaints and see what you can find.

2. The Marco Mindset

Marco is our most valuable customer. He is a regular customer, he proactively recommends us, and he helps us with new product development. His lifetime value to us is three times our average customer. When we deal with Marco we treat him like a king. Do you have any Marco customers? Do all of your frontline staff know who they are?

Every complaining or defecting customer is a potential Marco. They also have the potential to influence other Marcos. You never know who this person may know. Could their father-in-law be your best customer? We need to have the mindset that everyone we deal with could be a Marco when we are soliciting and listening to complaints.

When we have that Marco mindset, some amazing changes occur. Our body language opens up. We want to help. We are interested in their point of view. We automatically treat the person with a high level of respect. What is also amazing is that the complaining customer becomes easier to deal with, because they feel genuinely valued.

3. From Anger to Information

First Impressions

Secrets of Successful Complaint Handling

Turning Mr Angry around into someone who wants to sing your praises is a tough call. But it is possible. Here's your opening line:

"Mr Brown, I am so glad that you took the time and trouble to call me. This gives me a chance to hear exactly what happened and sort this out for you. I have some information here about what happened – would you tell me about your experience?"

Your message is "I'm on your side".

Continue to build rapport with your customer by empathizing with what he is feeling. This does not mean that you agree with what he says happened, you are agreeing that he is feeling angry, or upset, or frustrated.

Then close you mouth, open your ears and start writing. Listen actively. Paraphrase what he says so that you are really clear on how he feels and what he thinks happened.

Ask him more about how the staff treated him, get their names.

Language

The language and pace at which you talk can play a huge part in calming down the conversation. Your rapport building opening will set the tone for the conversation. If he is uptight and talking quickly, speed up your pace of talking too and gradually slow it down to a calmer tone. He will follow your lead.

Listen to the language he is using. Is he talking about facts or emotions? Is he clipped and business like or having an unruly outburst? Try to match the style of language slightly then gradually bring it to a calm, rational discussion about facts.

Body Language

Secrets of Successful Complaint Handling

When you are face to face, there are a number of things to remember about your body language:

Get on a level with your customer. If he is sitting, pull up a chair. If he is standing, stand next to him rather than directly opposite in a confrontational stance. [I'm on your side]

Use open gestures rather than crossing your arms or legs. [I want to hear what you have to say]

Lean forward and look attentive. [I am listening]

Look at him directly, paraphrase his point then note it down. [I am taking this seriously]

Even if you are talking on the phone, you can use body language to great effect.

When you make or take the call, stand up. This helps to control the conversation.

If you are sitting to take notes, lean forward as if you were talking to someone next to you.

Make sure you have a clear desk and your email is minimized. If you are distracted from the conversation, the customer will notice and get more upset.

Interest Level

When you are in the Marco mindset, you care. If you are supposed to be somewhere else, or if you don't think this customer is telling the truth or worth talking to, your interest level will drop. Showing that you are not that interested will have one of two outcomes:

1. This will turn into the longest, most drawn out complaint you have ever dealt with, or

2. The customer is going to walk away and never come back.

Secrets of Successful Complaint Handling

What You Need To Know

Here is the key information you need to collect before you call or approach the complaining customer:

The customer's full name with correct spelling and pronunciation

Contact details with any constraints e.g. prefer a call in the evening

What exactly has happened? Dig behind the surface of the story to get as many details as possible. What are the facts and what is opinion.

Who the customer has already spoken to and what that person / people committed to.

Your company policy or common practice in dealing with this situation.

The lifetime value of this customer. Recent transaction history, any unusual events.

Your options regarding service recovery or compensation.

As you talk with your customer, note down the main points that emerge. Out of courtesy, check that the customer doesn't mind you taking notes.

Check the contact details are correct.

What are the main points of the service failure, as the customer sees it.

Names of staff they dealt with, times and locations as appropriate.

What are the consequences of the service failure as the customer sees it. N.B. You are not offering to compensate for these consequences at this stage, but you need to in order to understand the customer's point of view.

Secrets of Successful Complaint Handling

Key points that you made.

Service recovery that was agreed on.

Any other actions that were agreed with deadlines.

This information is useful in case you need legal or insurance advice and will save time. It forms the basis of your letter to confirm your conversation with the customer.

This letter gives you another chance to apologise for the service failure, assure the customer how valued his custom is and to confirm the actions that you have agreed on.

N.B. All of your front line staff <u>need</u> the skills and confidence to handle complaints well. Have they got them?

Chapter 5: Give and Learn

You are fortunate enough that the customer has come to you with their complaint. Once you have heard the whole story, and have got a really clear idea of how the customer has been affected, you are ready to act. There are three things you need to give the customer:

1. A sincere apology,
2. Reassurance that you will do what it takes to make sure no one else will experience this problem and
3. Gesture of goodwill.

What is an appropriate gesture? You can ask the customer what he would like. You can offer a couple of alternatives. It should be something that is of high value to him and as low a cost to you as possible. It should also encourage the customer to keep using your firm.

          www.businessjigsaw.com

Secrets of Successful Complaint Handling

If your business is one where you can predict a high volume of complaints in the short term at least (e.g. transportation), then it is worth setting up contracts with suppliers of appropriate service recovery gifts. This could be as simple as a standard set of bouquets of flowers with your local florist. At British Airways, we arranged with our wine supplier to create special gift boxes of 3 bottles of fine wine. These ranged in value and quality according to whether the customer was a Blue, Silver or Gold member of our frequent flyer programme, Executive Club.

This doesn't have to stop you deciding on an individualized gift but it does make the process quicker and cheaper for your complaint handling team, as well as ensuring a consistent quality of gift for your customers.

Here are some examples of service recovery gestures that are high value to the customer, low cost to the company and encourage future custom.

Service Recovery Gestures

Hotel
Amount taken from your bill today
Free wine with your next meal
Free meal at our restaurant
Room upgrade for the rest of your stay / next stay

Telecommunications Company
Discount from your next bill
Free upgrade to the next package
Second phone line half price / free

Electronics Equipment Maintenance
Discount from your next bill
10% extra units in your next order free
Extra maintenance cycle at no extra cost

Professional Service Firm
Health check / Audit free
Reduction in fees for next bill

Secrets of Successful Complaint Handling

Complementary ticket for seminar

High Street Retailer
Refund on item plus new one free
Discount voucher for next visit

** All of your front line staff need to have the tools, empowerment, skills and confidence to use service recovery appropriately. Have they got them?

Learn from the Complaint

You also have to learn from the complaint case. Where did your processes break down? If it was something the customer failed to do, how can you educate customers in future, perhaps setting more realistic expectations? Have you got some kind of process for recording complaints with the reason and cost to handle? Are you analyzing the data to tackle the root causes?

1. Capture

Capture the complaints data in a form that can be easily summarized and analysed.

If you are using a complaints handling system (e.g. Respond) then it is easy to set up codes and categories for each complaint. These categories should relate to the customer experience definition (see Chapter 1). As each stage of the customer experience may cut across different silos or departments, it is critical to get enough detailed coding so that teams can be held accountable and get actionable feedback.

2. Review

Review complaint data at monthly management meetings. Ensure mitigating actions are in place to avoid reoccurrence.

In a truly customer focused organization, the CEO will make this a permanent agenda item at operational review meetings. Both the hard volumes and root cause data and the anecdotal quotations from letters or calls should be included.

3. Analyse

Analyse complaints data for root causes. Often this involves communication between departments so makes it a cross functional responsibility.

Some organizations put this analysis function in their Customer Relations Team. Others have a central Customer Insight team where this is just one source of customer data to be included in a wider picture, usually along with market research and usage or purchasing pattern information.

The important thing is that the highly valuable information about what customers think of your service is USED: to develop and improve products and services and to build customer loyalty.

4. Allocate Costs

Allocate realistic costs to the complaints. Handling costs and service recovery costs are relatively easy to identify. Add in the loss of future revenue, referrals and up sell revenue to get a better picture.

If your organization uses a CRM (Customer Relationship Management) system, it may provide a lifetime value score for that customer or customer segment. When a customer changes their purchasing behaviour as a result of a service failure, a revenue impact can be calculated. This cost, together with the cost of handling the complaint can be used in business cases to invest in or change a product or service.

As you reach the end of this book you will have the ideas, tools and techniques to make sure that your customer's views are listened to and acted on. Now you just have to sit back and watch your costs fall and your repeat revenue rise.

If you think you may need to improve the customer handling skills of your team, get in touch. At <u>Business Jigsaw</u> we offer in house courses as well as helping organisations revamp their complaint handling strategies.

<u>www.businessjigsaw.com</u>

Acknowledgements

I would like to thank all of my friends and colleagues who helped to encourage and support me in putting this book together. In particular:

To Caroline Connor, Head of Customer Complaints from BSKYB, who generously gave of her time and provided real life examples to my ideas.

To all of my former colleagues at Telewest Broadband, where we grappled with all of the legacy issues of the telecoms industry and brought customer focus to the forefront.

To my former colleagues at British Airways, especially those in the Customer Relations department. We had the advantage of a strongly customer focused culture but still had to fight hard with the technology and budget constraints to provide an outstanding service for our valued and valuable customers.

To Andy Byers, who has helped with the practical aspects of bringing the book to an audience, and to Andy Ferguson, who inspired me to avoid procrastination and just get on with it.

Finally, to my husband Mark who supported me all the way.

About the Author

Clare Moore runs a successful speaking, training and consultancy business called Business Jigsaw.

She comes from a family of entrepreneurs and broke with tradition by going to business school and then joining the graduate programme of a major airline. In her 9 years with BA, she worked in Operations, Sales, Marketing and managed the Customer Relations department as well as the customer service for BA's Frequent Flyer programme, "Executive Club". She then moved to be Head of Customer Relationship Management post with a large telecoms firm before starting Business Jigsaw.

How This Book Came About

Clare has always been passionate about the need for excellent customer service. In her work developing business skills with entrepreneurs and corporate employees, she noticed that while there was a lot of talk about customer service, there was still a huge amount of poor practice around complaint handling. Using her experience of working frontline in a variety of industries and of managing a large team who handled complaints, she has put together a practical guide to avoiding complaints and handling them to retain customers.

Services Available

At Business Jigsaw we can help your organization to improve your customer satisfaction and the way you handle complaints in four ways:

1. Consultancy and Knowledge Transfer
   Customer Service Strategy
   Customer Experience Management
   Complaint Handling Processes

2. Training Programmes
   Customer Service Skills – Telephone
   Customer Service Skills – Face to Face
   Customer Service Skills – Letter and Email
   Handling Difficult Customers Skills

3. Business Coaching
   Personal Performance
   Team Performance
   Performing Through Change
   Career Management

Secrets of Successful Complaint Handling

4. Keynote Speaker
   Clare Moore is a member of the
   Professional Speakers Association.

   Some of her most popular keynote
   topics are:
   • Finding and Keeping Profitable
     Customers
   • Turning Complaints into Gold Dust
   • Boosting Customer Satisfaction

See www.claremoore.co.uk for more details.

If you want to talk about how you could
improve your organisation's ability to
provide customer satisfaction and fantastic
complaint handling, contact us now by
emailing info@businessjigsaw.com
or calling +44 1786 834119.

www.businessjigsaw.com

Your   Notes..

Secrets of Successful Complaint Handling

Printed in the United Kingdom
by Lightning Source UK Ltd.
136390UK00002B/282/A